INSTEAD SAY THIS
FOR PARENTS OF ELEMENTARY SCHOOL CHILDREN

By Kishon M. Whittier, PsyD, LP

Instead Say This...
For Parents of Elementary School Children
Copyright © 2019 by Kishon M. Whittier
ISBN: 9781087817286

Dedicated to Meara, Reese, Van, and Joseph

for guiding, teaching, and training me

As our children grow older, they gain more independence. This can sometimes give us as parents an idea that our children don't need us as much. They do though, just in a different way. They need us to guide, teach, and train them so they can learn important competencies, including skills of daily living, how to manage emotions in a healthy way, and how to form and sustain relationships with others.

This parenting job can lead to much frustration and sometimes the words we use to guide, teach, and train our children do little to support their development in a positive way. However, there are words we can use that will feel better for both parent and child.

The format of this book is as follows: The page on the left is something we might say to our child. The page on the right offers an alternative that better supports our child's social-emotional development.

You've gotten this far, let's keep going.

Do you have any homework?

Instead say...

What homework do you have tonight?

You need to take a shower/bath. You smell.

Instead say…

Let's come up with a shower/bath schedule that we are both okay with.

I don't care if you are not tired, it's bedtime.

Instead say…

It's hard to go to bed when you are not feeling tired.

I am not buying you another hat. It's your fault you lost the other one.

Instead say…

I know you didn't try to lose your hat.
Let's decide how to keep track of your hat,
so that you are less likely to lose it next time.

I feel like a broken record and you never listen!

Instead say...

I would like to talk about this with you.
What is a way you can remember,
so it's your job and not mine to remind you?

It doesn't seem like you were trying very hard out there.

Instead say...

Were you feeling tired out there today?

Maybe you would have eaten a better dinner if you hadn't snacked so much after school.

Instead say…

That snack may have impacted your appetite for dinner. What is a reasonable time to stop snacking after school?

That's so gross that you didn't wash your hands after using the bathroom!

Instead say…

What is your understanding of why it's important to wash hands after using the bathroom?

I didn't see you all day. You should come grocery shopping with me.

Instead say...

I'd like to spend more time with you.
What should we plan to do together?

What's with the attitude?

Instead, say...

Seems like you are feeling upset about something. Was it a hard day today?

Some of the things you pick out to wear are so weird.

Instead say…

You have a unique style and it shows your fun personality!

You never listen to me.

Instead say...

I have something to say.
Let me know what you hear.

Are you mad at me?

Instead say…

You seem mad that you can't go to your friend's house.

That is a waste of your money. I wouldn't buy that.

Instead say…

It's up to you. It is your money
and you can choose what to spend it on.

Why am I always the one packing your bag for you?

Instead say...

I am sorry that I haven't given you a chance to get your own bag ready.
Does it work best for you to do that the night before or right before we leave?

Your room is such a mess!

Instead say…

It does not seem to bother you that your room is messy.
It does bother me though.
Is there a way we can compromise so we'd both be okay with it?

You never put things back after you use them.

Instead say…

I have a hard time finding things when they aren't put away. Would you be willing to try harder to put things away when you are finished using them?

Stop talking back to me.

Instead say...

I realize that when I talk to you disrespectfully, your response is to fight back. I will try to speak in a nicer tone to you.

Nope. That's not how you do it.

Instead say...

You are really working hard to figure that out.

You are so ungrateful.

Instead say...

This activity isn't really enjoyable for you. I was hoping it would be and it's okay that it didn't turn out the way I had hoped.

Just wait until your mom/dad gets home.

Instead say…

I am feeling really frustrated right now.
I need to take a break.

No.

Instead say…

I love you and the answer is no.

Can't you see I am in the middle of something?

Instead say…

I can answer that/help you in about five minutes.

Did you get in trouble today?

Instead say...

Tell me something that went well
and something that was hard today.

Say thank you to Grandma/Grandpa.

Instead say…

Is there anything you want to say to Grandma/Grandpa?

Are you listening to me?

Instead say...

It seems like you are not listening. I can wait until you are ready.

I really like that drawing you made.

Instead say...

Wow, I am noticing all the detail you put in that. Tell me about this drawing.

You are so good at math.

Instead say…

You worked really hard to finish that math worksheet.

I hate when I have to yell at you.

Instead say...

I am sorry. I was so mad, I yelled at you. I wish I would have taken a break and talked to you in a calmer way.

You have to wear your coat. It's cold outside.

Instead say…

You check the temperature outside
and decide what you need to wear to stay warm today.

I don't care who hit who first. We don't hit people.

Instead say...

What is something you could have done differently?

Be careful.

Instead say…

I'm here if you get stuck.

Share with your brother/sister.

Instead say…

It's okay if you don't want to share that right now.

I'll just do it.

Instead say...

Keep trying. I have faith you will figure it out.

Go to your room!

Instead say…

I think we both need a break right now.
Let's come back together when we aren't so mad.

I told you to put that away.

Instead say...

Please put that away before your next activity. Thanks.

You are so demanding!

Instead say…

It's hard to wait when you want something
and I'd appreciate if you asked me in a more respectful way.

You are being so loud.

Instead say...

You seem really excited/energetic.
However, that hurts my ears, could you take it down a notch?
Thanks!

I told you it was time to go. Why are you so mad about it?

Instead say…

It is hard to leave.
You really had fun here.
It's okay to be upset.

Don't talk back to me!

Instead say…

You must be really frustrated and I expect you to speak to me more respectfully.
Let's take a break and talk when we both feel better.

You love your sister/brother. Don't say that you don't.

Instead say…

Right now you are really mad at your sister/brother.

You can't be full. You barely ate anything. Take more bites.

Instead say...

If you feel full, trust your body.
If you get hungry later, you know the options
for a healthy snack.

But you like when I tease you about that. I can tell because you laugh.

Instead say…

I'm sorry. I got confused because you were laughing, but now I know you don't want me to tease you about that.
I will stop.

I worked really hard on cleaning the bathroom today and you're home for 5 minutes and it's trashed!

Instead say…

I am really disappointed. I cleaned the bathroom today and I feel disrespected because you left a mess after you used it.

You need to be done and start your homework.

Instead say...

What's your plan for homework tonight?

www.ingramcontent.com/pod-product-compliance
Lightning Source LLC
Chambersburg PA
CBHW060501010526
44118CB00018B/2491